DEADLY DISASTERS

Tornadoes

Disaster & Survival

Bonnie J. Ceban

Enslow Publishers, Inc.

40 Industrial Road	PO Box 38
Box 398	Aldershot
Berkeley Heights, NJ 07922	Hants GU12 6BP
USA	UK

http://www.enslow.com

Library of Congress Cataloging-in-Publication Data:

Ceban, Bonnie J.
    Tornadoes : disaster & survival / Bonnie J. Ceban.
        p. cm. — (Deadly disasters)
    Includes bibliographical references and index.
    ISBN 0-7660-2383-4
    1. Tornadoes—Juvenile literature. I. Title. II. Series.
  QC955.2.C43 2005
  363.34'923—dc22

                              2004011700

To Our Readers: We have done our best to make sure all Internet Addresses in this book were active and appropriate when we went to press. However, the author and the publisher have no control over and assume no liability for the material available on those Internet sites or on other Web sites they may link to. Any comments or suggestions can be sent by e-mail to comments@enslow.com or to the address on the back cover.

Illustration Credits: Associated Press, ANDERSON INDEPENDENT-MAIL, p. 38; Associated Press, AP, pp. 25, 27, 29, 31, 33, 34; Associated Press, CP, pp. 21, 23; Associated Press, TOPEKA CAPITAL-JOURNAL, p. 37; Enslow Publishers, Inc., p. 16; JIM REED/Science Photo Library, pp. 8, 11 (top); NOAA Photo Library, NOAA Central Library; OAR/ERL/National Severe Storms Laboratory (NSSL), pp. 1, 4, 11(bottom), 13, 14, 19, 40.

Cover Illustration: NOAA Photo Library, NOAA Central Library; OAR/ ERL/National Severe Storms Laboratory (NSSL)

Contents

After a funnel cloud drops down to the ground, a tornado has formed. Some tornadoes are narrow; some are very wide. Tornadoes can be very violent or somewhat weaker, but all of these storms are dangerous.

CHAPTER

Storm Clouds Over Mossy Grove

DELIGHTED LAUGHTER FILLED THE AIR IN MOSSY Grove, Tennessee. It was Sunday, November 10, 2002, and children were enjoying the unusually warm weather. It reached over 80°F. People were walking around town. Shopping malls were crowded. Parents watched children at the park.

However, soon the wind picked up, and cooler air blew through the town. Storm clouds quickly rolled in, catching many people off guard.

"It got real dark. Then [it] came across that ridge. This is the first place it touched down," Ken Jones explained his first look at the tornado. Jones, sixty-three, stood on his back porch. He watched the tornadoes form in the distance. He then rushed his wife and mother-in-law into the basement. Yet, he could not resist one more look.

He gazed at the approaching storm. "I got blown down the basement steps, if I had waited 30 seconds, I wouldn't be here."

The noise, like a roaring train whistle, bothered Jones the most. "Everything was just instantly gone. You wouldn't believe the power of that thing. It was a horrible noise. Then silence. Then the rain. When you look at the damage, it's a wonder anybody survived."[1]

A Line of Storms

Seventy tornadoes touched down that night. It was the worst outbreak of the season. The tornadoes ran from Louisiana to Pennsylvania. The National Weather Service called it one of the worst outbreaks on record. While the storms caused property damage, the real tragedy was the death toll. The storms claimed the lives of seventeen people in Tennessee, twelve in Alabama, and five in Ohio. In addition, Mississippi and Pennsylvania each lost one person. In total, thirty-six people died. Hundreds more were injured.

During the storm, Kevin Freels, of Mossy Grove was in awe. "I got the family in the tub, and there wasn't any room for me. So, I got beside it. The power went off, there was water everywhere. I realized that the roof came off. It felt like somebody was spraying me full force with a garden hose. When it was finally over, the tub was upside down but they were o.k."

Freels later examined the damage. He spoke of how lucky he felt. "That had to be God protecting us. I got to give Him credit. Because that's the only thing that saved us." As the storm had raged out of control, Freels realized that the only thing to do was to take cover in a safe place and hope for the best.[2]

Sticking Together

Another amazing event happened just blocks away. Since many of the area homes did not have basements, residents quickly came up with other options. For Fred and Susan Henry, that option was to run. Running through the street, they arrived at a neighbor's home. Together, the families took shelter.

Moments later, a Jeep and a car blew full force into the side of the house. The walls crumbled over the Henrys' seventeen-year-old daughter. The house began to peel away. Terror gripped the families. The storm continued over the now-open house. This time, the Henrys' nine-year-old son was picked up by the wind. Susan grabbed his ankles. Everyone else clung to Susan. Together they all held tight against the wind. The most amazing part of their story, though, is the ending. They all walked away with only minor injuries. The wind stripped much of their clothes away and a few pairs of shoes. It is a night they will remember forever—a night they never want to live through again.[3]

Death and Survival

Many families were not so lucky. Mike Williams Sr. did not survive the storm. It ripped apart his home and destroyed much of his block. His son, Mike Williams Jr., twenty-six, cried when he talked about his father. Mike saw his father just hours before the storms hit. The two had plans to get together the next day. Instead, it was a day spent in mourning. Families across the path of the storms suffered losses. Every state the storms touched lost at least one life.

This resident of Mossy Grove climbs over a wrecked house.

8

Emergency vehicles and personnel from the surrounding areas quickly made their way to the affected counties. Hundreds of injured, trapped, and missing people needed attention fast. Tommy Kilby was sad because of the casualties. He was also proud because the community pulled together. "We have been through a tremendous catastrophe. I've seen so much devastation and sorrow today. But, I've also seen a tremendous spirit. I've seen hope and thankfulness."[4]

Larry Schaefer, whose home was destroyed in the storms, was blessed by the community effort to help. A dozen men helped him move his furniture. They picked up pieces of the house. They also cleared paths for further work. "And only one of them is being paid," Schaefer, fifty-four, observed. "Those are all friends. They said 'Hey, if you want us to help, we will.'"[5]

Emergency aid, volunteer workers, and helpful neighbors abounded. The community of Mossy Grove, Tennessee, pulled together to rebuild their lives. However, thousands of homes were destroyed by the wind. Hundreds of businesses toppled, becoming piles of rubble. Most tragic, many lives were lost as the powerful storm tore through the counties. Perhaps less people would have died if they had understood how tornadoes worked.

CHAPTER 2

The Science of Tornadoes

A TORNADO IS ONE OF THE MOST POWERFUL windstorms on the entire planet. Its winds are packed tightly together. They rotate with great force. These funnel-shaped storm clouds cause the terrible losses of life that Mossy Grove experienced. How do these winds form? Can they be predicted? Scientists have asked these and other questions for a long time. Their research allows us to know some of the answers.

Prediction: Warnings and Watches

Certain types of weather make the conditions favorable for a tornado. A storm needs to be in a certain pattern. Scientists can look for storms that might bring tornadoes. They cannot always predict a tornado. But, when the right conditions for a tornado exist, they can tell if a storm could possibly create one.

A storm chaser observes a tornado in South Dakota (top). In the center of the radar at the bottom is something that meteorologists call a hook echo. A hook echo is often seen on a radar screen shortly before a tornado touches down.

When conditions exist for a tornado to form, a tornado watch is issued. The watch comes from the Storm Prediction Center in Norman, Oklahoma. It lets people know that a tornado could possibly touch down in the area. If a tornado watch is issued, people should get prepared.

If a tornado is spotted, a tornado warning is issued. The warning comes from the local National Weather Service office. Sometimes, the tornado is noticed on radar. Other times it is spotted on the ground by a storm chaser or other observer. Everyone within a warning area should quickly take shelter.[1]

Formation: How?

Scientists work very hard to discover exactly how tornadoes form. There are many ideas. No one knows exactly how it happens; however, they do know certain things. Tornadoes are always the result of a severe thunderstorm, which can have high winds and hail. Once a severe thunderstorm forms, it becomes possible for a tornado to begin forming. It is important to remember, though, that most thunderstorms do not result in tornadoes.[2]

The beginning formation of a tornado requires a spinning tube of air. That tube is formed by something called wind shear. Wind shear is the sudden change in the direction and speed of the wind. That spinning tube of air is cut by the storm's downdraft. A downdraft is the cooler air pressing down toward the ground. The spinning tube is then tilted into a column. The updraft, warmer air pushing up during the storm, will stretch the column into a full tornado. Depending on the size and strength of the tornado, it could last for a few seconds, minutes, or even an hour.[3]

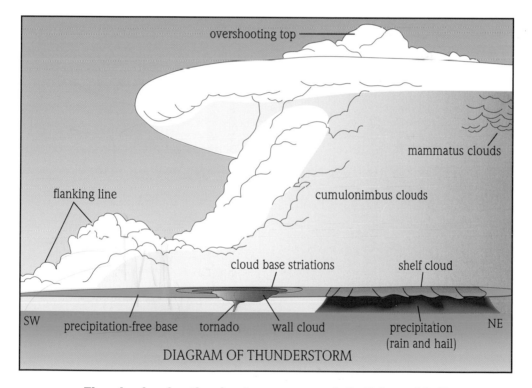

DIAGRAM OF THUNDERSTORM

The clouds of a thunderstorm are very tall. Rain and hail usually fall on the northeast side of storm. The southwest side has no precipitation. A tornado sometimes forms from a wall cloud on the southwest side of a storm.

A wall cloud (top) only forms during a thunderstorm. It lowers from a much larger cloud that does not contain rain. This rain-free cloud is usually south of the part of the storm where it is raining or hailing. Sometimes wall clouds rotate and then a tornado is possible. A funnel cloud (bottom) can drop down but does not become a tornado until it touches the ground.

Columns that form but do not touch the ground are called funnel clouds, and they are not considered tornadoes. However it is important to remember that a funnel cloud can turn into a tornado at any moment. So, they too should be treated with caution.[4]

Formation: Where?

Certain areas and countries have a much higher number of tornadoes every year than others. The United States is the country with the most tornadoes. There are about one thousand tornadoes in the United States during an average year.[5] Texas is the state with the most tornadoes with 124 a year.[6]

There is a part of the United States called "Tornado Alley." More thunderstorms form there than anywhere else in the world. It includes parts of Texas, Oklahoma, Kansas, Nebraska, Iowa, Colorado, South Dakota, Minnesota, and Wyoming.[7]

The second highest-rated tornado country is Canada. It averages 80 reported tornadoes per year.[8] While other areas of the world can and do have tornadoes, the midsection of the United States and Canada are by far the most likely places for a tornado to form.

Formation: When?

Tornadoes can form during any time of the year. They can also form at any time of the day. However, certain seasons

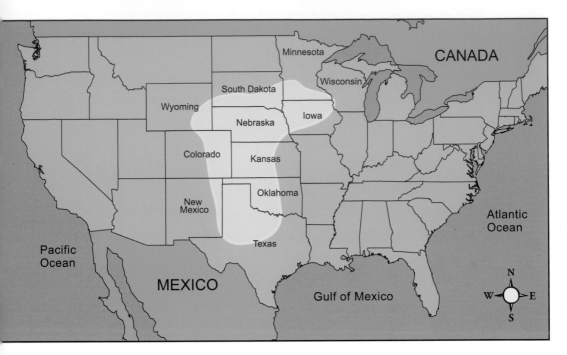

Tornado alley (in yellow) is the part of the United States that has the most tornadoes per year. The most violent tornadoes also occur there.

bring more tornadoes. Most tornadoes come between April and June, the highest amount in May. This is because of changes in air temperatures. The highest amounts of severe thunderstorms happen at that time. The fewest tornadoes occur in December and January.

Even though tornadoes can form any time of the day, they usually form late in the afternoon. That is when air is at its warmest. The largest number of tornadoes touches down between 4:00 and 6:00 P.M.

16

Strength: The Fujita Scale

Scientists measure the strength of a tornado on the six-point Fujita Scale (F–scale). Dr. T. Theodore Fujita was a meteorologist at the University of Chicago. He created the scale as a way for scientists to measure all tornadoes.

Fujita Scale		
Rating	**Wind Speed**	**Damage Level**
F0	Less than 73 mph	Light damage (some damage to chimneys; broken tree branches; shallow-rooted trees pushed over; sign boards damaged)
F1	73–112 mph	Moderate damage (roof tiles gone; automobiles blown off road)
F2	113–157 mph	Considerable damage (roofs torn off; large trees snapped or uprooted; cars lifted off ground)
F3	158–206 mph	Severe damage (roofs and some walls torn off; trains overturned; most trees uprooted; heavy cars lifted off ground and thrown)
F4	207–260 mph	Devastating damage (houses leveled; some houses blown off foundations; cars thrown)
F5	261–318 mph	Incredible damage (houses lifted off foundations and swept away; automobiles fly through air more than three hundred feet; bark stripped off trees)

Tornadoes that reach the F5 force are very rare. Whatever the rating, though, it is always necessary to be cautious and prepared for such a storm. One way to learn about tornadoes is to read about the experiences of those who have survived these storms.

CHAPTER 3

Camp Destruction

CAMPING SEASON WAS IN FULL SWING BY JULY 2000. Green Acres Campsite in Alberta, Canada, was nearly full. Over six hundred families had gathered. Some were there to enjoy the camping and fishing. Most were attending a baseball tournament. Everyone expected a fun time.

Early Friday evening, the camp was alive with activity. People were boating on the lake. Children played throughout the grounds. The smell of dinner floated across the campsites. The sun shone brightly. No one could have predicted what would happen next.

A Storm Approaches

A thunderstorm rolled quickly into the active camp. People began taking shelter from the rain. They were in

Hail can be very dangerous to drivers. It makes roads slippery and can break through windshields if the hail is very large.

camping trailers or tents. Others were still in boats. There were no solid shelters. It soon began to hail. Hail often comes before a tornado strikes. There was nowhere to go. The hail rained down. The people took shelter as best they could. Soon, the tornado hit. The twenty-minute storm brought a lifetime of damage.

A Camp Destroyed

In just twenty minutes, the campground was destroyed. Trailers were flattened. Boats were completely crushed

19

and cabins were destroyed. Twelve people were killed. One hundred thirty were injured.[1]

A policeman arriving on the scene said, "Trailers were tossed in the air like toys." He also said, "Trees were snapped like matchsticks." The tornado was classified as an F3. A local TV producer watching the scenes of destruction on television said, "It's like a war zone. Mobile homes upside down. People covered in blood. People carried out on stretchers."[2]

The Injured

One of those injured was six-year-old Devon Kline. The shelter of a trailer was not enough to keep Devon safe. A large tree branch whipped into his side. He suffered internal injuries. His spleen ruptured. He was taken to the hospital for surgery. Nearly a week later, he was able to go home. But, he was not over the storm. Devon became very afraid. He did not like being outside. Nature became scary for him. His mother, Darcy, explains, "He was even afraid of a leaf rustling. A slight breeze. Any leaf movement and he would not leave. 'I'm staying right here,' he'd say."[3]

Phyllis Galleberg, seventy-four, attempted to take shelter in her car. At the time, no one knew how bad the storm would become. As the tornado hit, she was stuck. The winds overtook her, and she was sucked from her car. Galleberg was thrown around by the force of the wind.

When rescue workers found her body, they thought she was dead. Leaving a blanket over her, they declared her victim number thirteen.

Soon, though, a campground employee heard a whimper from under the blanket. Quickly, he went for help. Galleberg was then airlifted to the hospital. Her injuries were significant. She went into a coma. She lost a leg and

The tornado at the Green Acres campground near Pine Lake took the campers by surprise. Here, three members of the search-and-rescue dive team look over the damage.

21

had to have many repairs to her skin. Yet, she came out of the coma and survived.

"What's done is done," says Galleberg. "If I sat here and cried, I would be crying alone. There's no point to that. There's still plenty to be thankful for." One thing she is thankful for is not remembering that day. Her injuries are her only reminder. "All my friends from the lake have visited. They told me all about it," she said. "I think it's good that I don't remember."[4]

A Camp Rebuilt

In total, there was $9 million in damage. It took over a year to rebuild the camp. When it opened, some survivors returned to the scene. Others could not. Devon Kline and his family returned. "We had to put some closure on a lot of things," said Darcy. Lexy Fisher, the owner, also needed to stop dwelling on the past. "It's time to go on and look forward. It gets to the point where you're ready to quit talking about it."[5]

Calgarian Michelle Gordon does not agree. Her rented cabin was crushed in the storm. She says, "No one is over it yet. No one can honestly say, 'that's it, I'm done.'" She made the decision not to return to the site. "I'm not going to put my family through that. It's not a memory I will ever want to deal with again."[6]

A difficult part of the storm was that it was unexpected.

Camping trailers were knocked on their sides when a tornado ripped through Green Acres campground in Canada.

Officials had posted a tornado warning. However, that warning did not reach the remote camp in time. Weather reports were not received. The vacationers had no time to prepare. The storm would have been destructive either way. Yet, it is always better to know what is coming. Currently, the camp is looking for better weather warning systems.[7]

23

Dark Horizon

THE TOWN OF JARRELL IS A SMALL FARMING COMMUNITY in a remote part of central Texas. Usually, it is a very quiet place. But there was nothing quiet there on May 27, 1997. A string of tornadoes ripped through the area. A few of those tornadoes even reached the rare force of F5. The storms left many casualties in their wake.

Only the Beginning

Ken Barner received a warning call from his neighbor. He ran for safety, but not before he saw the approaching storm. "It looked as bad as any of those tornadoes in the movie *Twister*. It looked like it could swallow up the whole town of Jarrell."[1]

The tornadoes arrived in the mid-afternoon. Many people were awed at the sight. "It was unbelievable," said

Thomas Soliz, "It was pretty frightening. You just look up and there it is."[2]

Mike Richardson, a storeowner in Jarrell, watched as a tornado formed. "The funnel was poking out of the sky. Then the dirt on the ground started to spin. Then the top and the bottom joined. You could see the tornado just start moving through town," he explained.[3] The twister moved through the center of town. It caused heavy damage to the buildings lining the streets. Cars parked on the street were destroyed. One grocery store lost its roof. Some buildings collapsed entirely.

A tornado moves across a field near Jarrell, Texas, on May 27, 1997.

Building Up Speed

At first the storm felt unreal to those watching. They stood staring in the parking lots as the tornado formed. Then, they realized what was happening. "It looked about two inches tall at first. Then is started taking up the entire horizon. It got closer, and building tops were flying around." Ray Westphal explained, "It was picking up cars right into the air, flinging them everywhere." Westphal manages a Wendy's restaurant in town. His parking lot was one where many gathered to watch. Until, "the funnel started coming through the sky—then everyone panicked."[4]

Searching Through the Rubble

Billy Dean Williams is a former Coast Guard officer. He watched the scene unfold from his front porch. "It came right up and then came back down. Then it came back up again. When it came down, all the clouds came together in a big black line," he explained.[5] Williams, along with his seventeen-year-old son, rushed to the area where they saw the twister touch down. Arriving, they found only flattened homes and absolute chaos. The two quickly worked to search for victims. They came upon six people dead in the wreckage. Soon, emergency vehicles began arriving. They poured into the neighborhood and quickly raced victims to waiting doctors at the town's hospitals.

Stepping back from the chaos in front of him, Williams

observed what happened. "It took every house on County Road 305, we had a big recycling plant and it's gone. Where there used to be houses, it looks like nothing is there. Just piles of rubble." By the time it was done, the twister leveled nearly a fourth of the town. It left its mark on almost all of it.[6]

Lost and Found

The day of disaster brought a big problem with missing people. All over, desperate families searched for loved ones. When nightfall started to descend, something

This disaster relief center was set up at Jarrell High School. Red Cross volunteers helped the local residents.

had to be done. Law officers requested family members come to Jarrell High School. There, they would be able to search the crowds and receive help. Relief and rescue missions were set up. Food and blankets were supplied.

"We have no idea how many people are out there," said Williamson County Deputy R. B. Raby. "It looks like somebody took a bulldozer out there to start a new subdivision. There's nothing left but pasture."[7] Those who gathered at the high school were able to rest. Many also helped with the relief efforts.

Some families were able to find one another at the school. Others had connected earlier in the day. By nightfall, though, some family members were still looking for each other. Three teenage girls arrived at a downtown checkpoint, nearly hysterical, looking for their mothers. "Where are they? Where are they? You must know! Where can we find them? We haven't talked to them for hours," one girl yelled. Tears were visible on all of their faces. The officers had no information to give. One officer took them to the high school. They were able to search for, and later find, their mothers.[8]

The intensity of the storm kept people scattered. The surprising arrival left little time to make emergency plans. While many families had reunions at the high school, many others were left wondering. It was a night of confusion—a night of missing persons.

Damage Done

When the storms died down, damage reports began to trickle in. Millions upon millions of dollars would be required to rebuild. The area was quickly declared a national disaster. Over one hundred homes were leveled. Dozens of businesses collapsed. The recycling plant was destroyed.

The most difficult damage number, though, was the death toll. Over thirty people lost their lives. Of those people, seven were children. The devastation of that news shocked Janine Brock. She lived in Jarrell her whole life. "I thought the one in 1989 was awful. But, this is worse. It's going to be awful. They're going to have to bury so many people."[9]

No city wants to have to mourn so many people. But Midwest communities sometimes fall victim to these powerful storms. In 1999, Oklahoma City would have to mourn some victims of its own.

Most of Jarrell, Texas, was completely flattened by the devastating tornado.

CHAPTER

5

Twenty Tornadoes

EARLY ON MAY 3, 1999, WEATHER REPORTS IN THE Oklahoma City, Oklahoma area indicated that the chance of storms was growing. Then, at 3:00 P.M., a severe thunderstorm warning was issued for the area that included Moorland High, an Oklahoma City suburb. Shirley Phillips understood the meaning. For her, the warning meant it was time to get her children inside and prepare for the coming storms.

The first warning alarms sounded at 4:30 P.M.[1] The storms hit only moments after the alarms sounded. Many people were stunned by what happened next. That night, twenty tornadoes touched down. Seven of those tornadoes reached F5 force. In total, forty-five people were killed. More than five hundred others were hospitalized. The damage was much worse than could have been predicted.[2]

Tammy Holngren and her children take shelter under a highway overpass near Newcastle, Oklahoma. All three were uninjured. However, it is unsafe to take cover under an overpass during a tornado. Winds actually pick up speed when they move under an overpass. If one is caught on the highway, it is better to lie down in a deep ditch.

The Phillips Home

The storm's force arrived quickly at Oklahoma City and the surrounding area. Shirley Phillips is a longtime resident of this region. Along with Phillips, two adults and two children were home. The group prepared quickly. They tucked themselves into a bedroom closet and waited. Phillips recalls, "Right before it hit, everything got real quiet. Dark. Then came this huge roar. The bedroom windows shattered. I looked up and saw this swirling in the bedroom." Phillips' roof ripped off, creating big swirling winds through the house. It swirled everything from furniture to food. Still, the storm raged on. Frightened, the children grew more upset. "I must have sung 'Precious Memories' to my babies four or five times to keep them calm," Phillips explained.

The end of the storm meant examining the damage. All that remained of Phillips' home was one closet frame. That frame kept the family protected from the winds. "Looking at all that mess, I feel very lucky," Phillips said, knowing it could have been worse.[3]

> ". . . everything got real quiet. Dark. Then came this huge roar."
>
> —Shirley Phillips, tornado survivor

Survival of the Shannons

Just a few blocks away from the Phillips family, Trina Shannon and her infant daughter fought to keep shelter. The storm hit hard and Shannon had little time to prepare. Quickly, she raced with her daughter to find protection. As she ran, she caught a look at the storm. "I had seen that tornado jump across 1-35, so big. So black and wide." Shannon had few options. The home had no basement. Instead, she crawled with her daughter beneath a mattress placed over the bathtub. The tub rattled, the baby cried, and the walls bulged, but the bathroom stood strong.[4]

The 1999 tornado that hit Oklahoma City was a half a mile wide.

The storm hit as Shannon's husband drove home. He fought traffic, rushing toward his family. He knew his wife and daughter were in the storm's force. Panicked, he arrived to the scene. The roads remained closed. Miles later, he was able to pull off the road. He hurried to his house. His legs ached from running. Relieved, he found his wife and daughter in the front yard. Power lines and wreckage were everywhere. For this family, the reunion was a happy one. They were all safe and together again.

33

Yet, the storm did not come without cost. The Shannons' home was destroyed. And, with no insurance, they would be unable to rebuild. They would have to wait for the government to help. "Well, we've got to start all over," Trina said with sorrow as she stood in what was once their front yard.[5]

After the rampaging tornado in Oklahoma City, rescue workers and neighbors dig through the rubble to try to find a missing woman on May 3, 1999.

The Agony of Separation

Craig Denny grew concerned. At work, he watched the WeatherData radar screen. His job is to issue weather warnings for the local area. He watched as the storms approached his home and as the tornadoes touched down in his neighborhood. "I was too busy to call home because I had so many warnings to issue," Denny explained.[6]

The evening was stressful and hectic. Being separated from his family was difficult. Focusing on the work was a test of commitment. A half hour after the tornado hit, Denny received a call from his wife. Everything at home was all right. "It's really tough working when you know the weather is literally hitting your own back yard," Denny said. People like Denny understand the importance of getting their jobs done so that lives can be saved.[7]

6

Staying Safe

TORNADOES ARE A FRIGHTENING EVENT. YET, THERE are ways to try to keep people safe. Always be aware of the best safety measures. Be alert to warnings. Know the threat. Then, get prepared.

Predictions

In the United States, the National Weather Service gives tornado forecasts. Always pay attention to these forecasts. There are two kinds. During a tornado watch, keep your radio on for more information. Always listen for possible tornado warnings. A warning gives you time to prepare. A warning usually lists the possible towns and cities that the tornado could strike.[1]

Plans

It is always a good idea for a family to have a plan of action, even in areas where tornadoes are not as frequent. A plan

Many homes in tornado alley have a tornado shelter that is underground. These shelters are often made of concrete and have a door that can be chained shut.

will make sure that everyone knows what to do. Preparedness is always a good idea.

The best plan of action is to get to a basement or underground tornado shelter. Get there quickly. Take shelter under mattresses, heavy furniture, or thick sleeping bags. They offer protection from flying debris such as shards of broken glass. If there is no basement, a safe room should be designated. It should have no windows. It should be toward the center of the house. A closet, bathroom, or laundry area can work. Everyone needs to know in advance.

Mobile homes are not safe in tornadoes. The best plan is to leave. Mobile homes are too easily destroyed. They are often flipped over. Many mobile-home neighborhoods have an underground tornado shelter for the residents.

Students at Powdersville Middle School in South Carolina practice a tornado drill. They crouch in the hallway with textbooks over their heads for protection. Some schools have tornado shelters or basements, both of which are safer than hallways.

Otherwise, it is best to get to a building with a permanent foundation. The tornado plan should include exactly where to go as well as the fastest way to get there. Then, family members will know where to find one another. When there are plans, people are less likely to panic.[2]

Sometimes tornadoes will strike when people are not at home. Plans should include these situations. Office buildings, schools, hospitals, and shopping malls should all have tornado emergency plans. It is important to know what they are.

A family check-in person is also a good idea. This is a

family member or friend from another area. Everyone can call this person after the storm. The family check-in person will be responsible to make contacts as quickly as possible.[3]

Knowledge

Tornado predictions are not perfect. Storms develop quickly. Warnings do not always reach everyone in time. It is good to know some signs of a tornado.

If there is rotation in the thunderstorm clouds, a tornado may be forming. Another sign is swirling dust on the ground. These signal that the rotating wind is reaching downward. Sound is also important. A loud and persistent rumble that does not fade can indicate an approaching tornado. It is much louder than normal wind or thunder. Some compare it to the sound of a nearby train.[4]

> **"It was picking up cars right into the air, flinging them everywhere."**
>
> **—Ray Westphal, tornado survivor**

These signs should not create panic. Remember most thunderstorms pass by without tornadoes ever touching down. It is always smart to be alert. If you see a sign of a tornado, take precautions. Always get to a protected place.

Storm Chasers

One of the best ways researchers have found for studying storms is to go find them. Storm chasers are special researchers. They seek storms that might produce tornadoes.

A member of Project Vortex films a storm that could possibly produce tornadoes. Vortex stands for Verification of the Origins of Rotation in Tornadoes EXpermiment. The group from the National Severe Storms Laboratory hopes to learn as much as they can about the conditions for the formation of tornadoes.

They follow the storms. Then, they follow any tornadoes. Howard Bluestein has been a storm chaser since the 1970s. He works with the research program at the University of Oklahoma. "I wouldn't do it if it were dangerous. We believe we understand the storms and we do not put ourselves in any danger of being hit by a tornado. The biggest danger is the country roads. The other is lightning,"

Bluestein explains. However, Bluestein is a professional, and no one should ever try to chase tornadoes unless he or she is trained to do so.[5]

A storm chaser's job has changed over time. In the 1970s, storm chasers helped develop Doppler radar systems. They could see the storm and forecasters could see the screen. Together, they discovered what pictures on the screen meant the storm was doing. Later, they began studying tornado formation. They also use weather balloons. Storm chasers have helped create new research. This improves technology and warning systems and saves lives.[6]

Bluestein has seen these storms up close. He has seen the strength of them. He has also seen the destruction. While people should always be prepared and alert of the dangers, he also thinks they should be awed. Bluestein observes, "Nature is incredibly powerful."[7]

> "Where there used to be houses, it looks like nothing is there. Just piles of rubble."
>
> —Billy Dean Williams, tornado survivor

41

Top Ten Deadliest Tornadoes in the United States

Rank	Date	Place	Deaths	Magnitude
1	March 18, 1925	Missouri, Illinois, and Indiana	695	F5
2	May 7, 1840	Louisiana and Natchez, Mississippi	317	*
3	May 27, 1896	St. Louis, Missouri and Illinois	255	F4
4	April 5, 1936	Tupelo, Mississippi	216	F5
5	April 6, 1936	Gainesville, Georgia	203	F4
6	April 9, 1947	Texas, Oklahoma, and Kansas	181	F5
7	April 24, 1908	Louisiana and Mississippi	143	F4
8	June 12, 1899	New Richmond, Wisconsin	117	F5
9	June 8, 1953	Flint, Michigan	115	F5
10	May 11, 1953	Waco, Texas	114	F5

*The Fujita Scale was developed in 1971. However, tornadoes that occurred prior to 1971 were still rated based on the damage that they caused. Unfortunately, there was not enough damage on record for the May 7, 1840 tornado to determine an accurate Fujita rating.

Chapter Notes

Chapter 1. Storm Clouds Over Mossy Grove

1. J. J. Stambaugh, "Storm-shattered lives; Rescue teams optimistic as search resumes," *Knoxville News-Sentinel*, November 12, 2002, p. A1.

2. David M. Halbfinger, "A Trail of Destruction At least 36 Dead in the Aftermath of 66 Tornadoes," *The New York Times*, November 12, 2002, p. A1.

3. Ibid.

4. Ibid.

5. Ibid.

Chapter 2. The Science of Tornadoes

1. Jack Williams, *The Weather Book* (New York: Vintage Books, 1997), p. 87.

2. Roger Edwards, "Tornado Forecasting," *The Online Tornado FAQ*, n.d., <http://www.spc.noaa.gov/faq/tornado/#Forecasting> (September 20, 2004).

3. Williams, p. 89.

4. "Questions and Answers About Tornadoes," *National Severe Storms Laboratory*, August 23, 2004, <http://www.nssl.noaa.gov/edu/tornado> (September 20, 2004).

5. "Tornadoes," *NOAA*, June 10, 2004, <http://www.noaa.gov/tornadoes.html> (July 9, 2004).

6. "Annual Average Number of Tornadoes, 1950–1995," *NCDC: Tornadoes*, July 1, 2004, <http://www.ncdc.noaa.gov/img/climate/severeweather/small/aug+5095.gif> (July 9, 2004).

7. Williams, p. 89.

8. "Tornadoes," *Environment Canada*, June 2, 2004, <http://www.pnr-rpn.ec.gc.ca/air/summersevere/ae00s02.en.html> (July 9, 2004).

Chapter 3. Camp Destruction

1. Carol Harrington, "Pine Lake Haunted by Tornado Memories," *The Canadian Press*, December 27, 2000, p. A1.

2. "Tornado wrecks Canadian campsite," *BBC News*, July 15, 2000, <news.bbc.co.uk/hi/english/world/americas/newsid_834000/834669.stm> (September 20, 2004).

3. Harrington, p. A1.

4. Ibid.

5. Ibid.

6. Ibid.

7. Susan Kim, "Canada Tornado Death Toll Rises," *Disaster News Network*, July 15, 2000, <http://www.disasternews.net/disasters/7-17-00_canada_death_toll.shtml> (September 20, 2004).

Chapter 4. Dark Horizon

1. Bill Hanna, "Storms' Rage kills 32," *Fort Worth Star-Telegram*, May 28, 1997, p. 1.

2. The Associated Press, "Twister Kills at Least 30," *Amarillo Globe-News*, ©1996, <http://www.amarillonet.com/stories/052897/twister.html> (October 19, 2004).

3. Ibid.

4. Chip Brown, "Tornadoes Kill 19 in Texas," *South Coast Today*, May 28, 1997, <http://www.s-t.com/daily/05-97/05-28-97/a08wn030.htm> (October 19, 2004).

5. Hanna, p. 1.

6. Ibid.

7. Ibid.

8. Ibid.

9. "Tornado Aftermath," *Lubbock Avalanche-Journal*, ©1997, <http://www.lubbockonline.com/news/052997/tornado.htm> (October 19, 2004).

Chapter 5. Twenty Tornadoes

1. Lee Hill Kavanaugh, "Slight Chance of Storms, then . . . Death dropped from the sky," *The Kansas City Star*, May 5, 1999, p. A1, metropolitan edition.

2. Rick Montgomery, "We've got to Start Over," *The Kansas City Star*, May 5, 1999, p. A19.

3. Rhonda Chriss Lokeman, "Picking up the Lives Splintered by the Storm," *The Kansas City Star*, May 9, 1999, p. K3.

4. Ibid.

5. Ibid.

6. Ibid.

7. Ibid.

Chapter 6. Staying Safe

1. Roger Edwards, "Tornado Forecasting," *The Online Tornado FAQ*, n.d., <http://www.spc.noaa.gov/faq/tornado/#Forecasting> (September 20, 2004).

2. Roger Edwards, "Tornado Safety," *The Online Tornado FAQ*, n.d., <http://www.spc.noaa.gov/faq/tornado/#Safety> (September 20, 2004).

3. "Tornadoes . . . Nature's Most Violent Storms," National Severe Storms Laboratory, September 1992, <http://www.nssl.noaa.gov/NWSTornado/> (September 20, 2004).

4. Roger Edwards, "Tornado Forecasting."

5. Jack Williams, *The Weather Book* (New York: Vintage Books, 1997), p. 96.

6. Ibid.

7. Ibid., p. 98.

Glossary

Fujita Tornado Scale—System used for rating the severity of tornadoes.

funnel cloud—A rotating column of air extending from a cloud. A funnel cloud that reaches the ground is called a tornado.

National Weather Service—The service which studies weather patterns, research, and formation. They also issue weather watches and warnings.

severe thunderstorm—A thunderstorm with winds 58 mph or faster or with hailstones three-fourths of an inch or larger.

tornado—A strong, rotating column of air extending from the base of a thunderstorm cloud to the ground.

tornado warning—Alert issued from local branches of the National Weather Service indicating that a tornado is nearby.

tornado watch—Alert issued from the National Weather Service indicating potential tornado activity.

water spout—A tornado that occurs over water, pulling the water up into the rotating winds.

Further Reading and Internet Addresses

Books

Allaby, Michael. *Tornadoes*. New York: Facts on File, Inc., 2004.

Berger, Melvin and Gilda. *Do Tornadoes Really Twist?* New York: Scholastic Inc., 2000.

Challoner, Jack. *Eyewitness: Hurricanes and Tornadoes*. New York: Dorling Kindersley Publishing, 2000.

Osbourne, Will and Mary Pope Osbourne. *Twisters and Other Terrible Storms*. New York: Random House, 2003.

Rupp, Rebecca. *Weather*. North Adams, Mass.: Storey Kids, 2003.

White, Matt. *Storm Chasers: On the Trail of Deadly Storms*. Mankato, Minn.: Capstone Press, 2003.

Internet Addresses

National Oceanic and Atmospheric Administration (NOAA) Home Page—Tornadoes
<http://www.noaa.gov/tornadoes.html>

Tornado Project Online
<http://www.tornadoproject.com>

Tornado Safety Tips
<http://www.crh.noaa.gov/mkx/owlie/tornado1.htm>

Index